SMART ABOUT

History

The Pilgrims and ME

by Carrie Rosen

by Judy Donnelly
illustrated by
Maryann Cocca-Leffler
Grosset & Dunlap · New York

For Carol—JD

Lots of hugs to my models:
Kristin, my "Pilgrim" daughter and Eric, my sleepy husband.
Thanks for being such good sports!—MC-L

Page 13 photo of Plymouth Rock by Don Teague, Destination Plymouth. All other photographs by Maryann Cocca-Leffler.

Text copyright © 2002 by Judy Donnelly. Illustrations copyright © 2002 by Maryann Cocca-Leffler. Reprinted by arrangement of Grosset & Dunlap, a division of Penguin Young Readers Group, a member of Penguin Group(USA)Inc.All rights reserved. Published by Grosset & Dunlap, a division of Penguin Putnam Books for Young Readers, 345 Hudson Street, New York, NY 10014. GROSSET & DUNLAP is a trademark of Penguin Putnam Inc. Published simultaneously in Canada. Manufactured in China

Library of Congress Cataloging-in-Publication Data

Donnelly, Judy.
     The Pilgrims and me / by Judy Donnelly ; illustrated by Maryann Cocca-Leffler.
        p. cm.
     Summary: Examines the history of the Pilgrims and how they came to settle in America, in the form of a class report.
     1. Pilgrims (New Plymouth Colony)—History—Juvenile literature. 2. Pilgrims (New Plymouth Colony)—Social life and customs—Juvenile literature. 3. Massachusetts—History—New Plymouth, 1620-1691—Juvenile literature. 4. Massachusetts—Social life and customs—To 1775—Juvenile literature. [1. Pilgrims (New Plymouth Colony) 2. Massachusetts—History—New Plymouth, 1620-1691.] I. Cocca-Leffler, Maryann, 1958– ill. II. Title.
F68.D64   2002
974.4′8202—dc21
                                                                                                      2002004664

ISBN 0-448-42699-4 (pbk)   A B C D E F G H I J
ISBN 0-448-42883-0 (GB)   A B C D E F G H I J

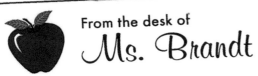

From the desk of
Ms. Brandt

Dear Class,
  We have been learning about so many exciting events from the past. Now you may choose a subject that is of special interest to you for your report.
  You may write about something that happened thousands of years ago or about something that happened not so very long ago - maybe when your parents or your grandparents were your age. It's up to you!

  Here are some questions you might want to think about:

🍎 What made you pick your topic?

🍎 Did you learn anything that really surprised you?

Good luck and have fun!

Ms. Brandt

Unboring Pilgrims

Last fall my family took a trip to Plimoth Plantation. It is a special museum in Massachusetts. Going there was like being a time traveler. I saw just what it was like to live the way the Pilgrims did—almost 400 years ago.

Before my trip all I knew was that the Pilgrims had something to do with Thanksgiving. I thought that learning about them might be boring, but it wasn't.

At Plimoth Plantation I found out a lot about the Pilgrims. That's why I picked them for my report.

Be of good cheer!

Umm... Thanks!

I even met some Pilgrims. Well, kind of. They were guides dressed up in Pilgrim clothes. They even talked and acted the way the Pilgrims did.

America?

Before they came to America, the Pilgrims lived in England. They weren't happy there. They weren't allowed to pray the way they wanted to. They couldn't teach their religion to their children.

Across the ocean in America, the Pilgrims would be able to do whatever they wanted. They'd be all on their own. But were they brave enough to go? America was just forests and beaches. There were scary stories about it.

But finally the Pilgrims decided they would do it. They would make a new home in America.

Packing for the Trip

Deciding what to take wasn't easy.
The Pilgrims needed to bring tons of
things—there were no stores in America.
But there was not going to be much
room on the ship.

The Mayflower

The Pilgrims sailed on a ship called the *Mayflower*. They left England on September 6, 1620. Not counting the sailors, there were 102 people on board. About twenty were kids.

The ship was small. It was very crowded. The Pilgrims slept on the floor. The richer Pilgrims got the best spots.

Lower Deck
This is where the Pilgrims stayed.

The Forecastle
Sailors slept here.

The Windlass
It raised the anchor.

There was no water for baths or laundry, so most people wore the same clothes for the whole trip! There was no bathroom, either. Everybody used a pot. The ship was named for a flower, but it got really smelly.

The Round House where they kept maps and charts.

The Helm where they steered the ship.

The Great Cabin The Captain's room.

The Gun Room

The Hold where all the supplies were kept.

Crossing the Ocean

The trip to America was terrible. There were big storms and the Pilgrims got seasick. Water leaked on them, so they were cold and wet all the time. They mostly ate hard bread, dried fish, and cheese. Yuck!

There was nothing to do. It must have been sooo boring. The trip took sixty-six days. I get crazy if I'm in a car for an hour!

On our trip I took this picture of the *Mayflower II*. The ship is a copy of the real *Mayflower*. I went inside. It was cold and dark. I was surprised how small it was. I can't believe 102 Pilgrims squeezed on that ship.

Man overboard!

They left England Sept. 6, 1620

One Pilgrim fell overboard. They saved him!

Europe

They Made It!

On November 11, 1620, the Pilgrims landed at Cape Cod, Massachusetts. Finally they could get off the ship! The shore looked cold and wild. How could they live in this place?

LAND!

I bet the Pilgrims wouldn't believe that today millions of people come to Cape Cod for vacations. My family has been there twice.

↗ My sister and me on Cape Cod last summer.

Plymouth Rock

The Pilgrims finally found a good place to start a village. It was called Plymouth. An old story says that when the Pilgrims first came ashore, they stepped on a big rock—Plymouth Rock.

They used a small boat called a shallop to get from the Mayflower to the land.

Plymouth Rock used to be much bigger, but tourists chipped off pieces of it for souvenirs. Now it's under glass. →

The Pilgrims spelled 'Plimoth' lots of ways. They didn't care much about spelling!

Plymouth Rock ↙

1620

All Alone and Scared

The first winter in the new land was awful. Almost everybody lived on the *Mayflower* while the men worked on the first house. It took twenty-six days to build. Then it caught fire.

The weather was cold and stormy. There was hardly anything to eat. Almost everyone got sick. Half the Pilgrims died. They were buried at night. The Pilgrims were afraid that the Indians would attack if they knew how few Pilgrims were still alive. They must have felt like giving up and going back to England. But nobody did. I think they were really brave.

My Favorite Pilgrims

Here is something cool. Each guide at Plimoth Plantation pretends to be a real person who lived in the village. They all act as if they've never heard of cars or TV or anything modern. I met Myles Standish the day I was there. He's one of my favorite Pilgrims.

William Bradford

He was the Pilgrim leader. He was a great person. He kept a journal—if he hadn't, we'd know hardly anything about the Pilgrims.

Constance Hopkins

She was ten. She had a big brother and a little sister, like I do. When she grew up, Constance had twelve children.

Francis and John Billington

Francis was ten and John was six. The two brothers got into lots of trouble. Francis made firecrackers with gunpowder and almost blew up the *Mayflower*! John got lost in the woods for five days. Some Indians brought him home. They even gave him beads to wear.

Captain Myles Standish

He was the only Pilgrim who had been a soldier. He was going to be in charge if there were any fights with the Indians. He had red hair and a hot temper.

Peregrine White

He was the first Pilgrim baby born in America. I love babies.

HOME!

By April life got better for the Pilgrims. They had built four houses at Plymouth. The houses were tiny—just one room for the whole family. The roofs were covered with dried grass. That's why the first house caught fire.

At Plimoth Plantation, there were lots of little houses like this one. I went inside a few. It was always dark, and usually there wasn't a lot furniture.

The beds were small. But people were shorter back then. ↓

I dressed as a Pilgrim for Halloween. ⤳

Don't bother looking for a toilet. They used a pot.

Not-So-Scary Indians

In England the Pilgrims had heard terrible stories about the Indians in America. At Plymouth they were very scared that the Indians would attack them. But guess what! One day an Indian walked right into town and said, "Welcome." The Pilgrims could hardly believe it. This Indian was friendly, and he spoke English!

The Pilgrims were embarrassed that the Indian wore hardly any clothes, so they gave him a red coat.

At Plimoth Plantation I saw a home just like the ones that the Indians lived in. It was made of tree bark. →

chief Massasoit →

Squanto →

The Pilgrims gave him presents, and he came back with more Indians. One was named Squanto. Through Squanto the Pilgrims met the most important Indian chief around. His name was Massasoit. He and the Pilgrims promised that they would never fight against each other. They stuck to it.

The Pilgrims' Best Friend

Squanto was my favorite Indian. He turned out to be the best friend the Pilgrims ever had. Squanto taught the Pilgrims how to plant corn. He also taught them to catch fish, find plants that were safe to eat, and make maple syrup. Without Squanto, more Pilgrims would have died.

Squanto spoke really good English. He had even been to England. Squanto had no family, so he acted as though the Pilgrims were his family. He liked them so much he came to live at Plymouth.

Work, Work, Work!

As time went by, the weather got better and more Pilgrims came from England. It was spring and there was a lot of work to do. The Pilgrims worked nearly all the time, even the kids. (My mother read my report, and she says I have it easy. All I have to do is set the table, empty the trash, and walk the dog.)

We're growing vegetables.

I picked long grass for our floor

I got water from the broo

I'm stuffing a mattress with pine needles.

I'm feeding the chicke

There was no school. Parents taught the children how to read and write.

The only day they didn't work was Sunday. Then the Pilgrims went to church and prayed. That is why they came to America in the first place.

Giving

By the next fall, seven houses were built. The Pilgrims had been in America almost a year now. There was plenty of food. Squanto and the Indians were their friends. And the Pilgrims could pray the way they wanted to. There was a lot to be thankful for, so they decided to have a big feast and invite Massasoit. They asked him to bring some friends. He showed up with ninety Indian men!

Thanks

The Pilgrims were afraid there wouldn't be enough food, but Massasoit was a good guest. He sent his men out hunting and they came back with five deer.

The first Thanksgiving wasn't one day. It lasted three whole days! The Pilgrims had it outside, like a big picnic. Eating wasn't all they did. They played games and had a parade with drums and a trumpet. No Indian women came. Neither did any Indian kids. But I put them in my picture anyway.

Pilgrim Manners

The Pilgrims thought it was good manners to eat with your fingers. That's probably why they had giant napkins. They didn't know about germs so everybody shared dishes and cups. Forks were a new invention for rich people. The Pilgrims didn't use them. They did have knives and spoons—sometimes the spoons were made of clamshells.

Pilgrims used giant napkins.

Pilgrim kids ha to stand durin meals.

The Truth About the First Thanksgiving

I always thought the Pilgrims ate just what people today have for Thanksgiving dinner, but that is not true. No one knows for sure whether the Pilgrims even had turkey. There was no cranberry sauce, either. Cranberries are sour, and the Pilgrims didn't have anything to make cranberries taste sweet. They made pumpkin pudding and pumpkin soup, but no pumpkin pie. The Pilgrims only ate pies filled with meat.

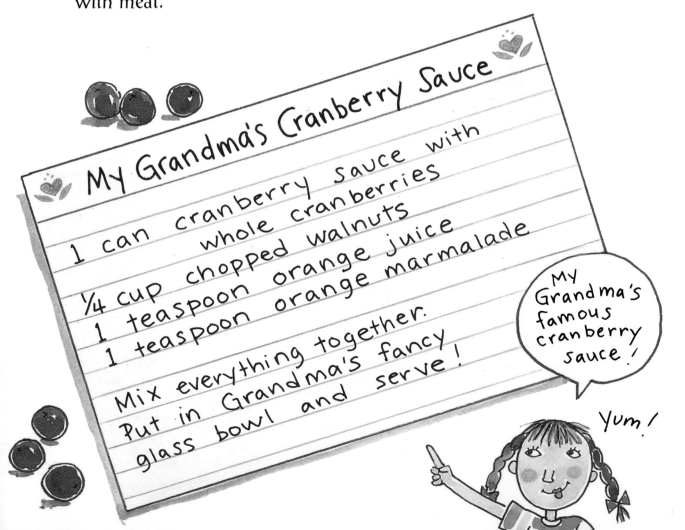

My Grandma's Cranberry Sauce

1 can cranberry sauce with whole cranberries
¼ cup chopped walnuts
1 teaspoon orange juice
1 teaspoon orange marmalade

Mix everything together.
Put in Grandma's fancy glass bowl and serve!

My Grandma's famous cranberry sauce!

Yum!

If the Pilgrims Came to

The Pilgrims would have loved Thanksgiving at my house. I sure love it. In the morning the house smells of turkey. Grandma and Grandpa come. I set the table. We put out the decorations that I made in first grade.

We always have mashed potatoes and sweet potatoes, corn pudding, a big salad, and Grandma's cranberry sauce. For dessert we have apple pie and pumpkin pie with vanilla ice cream. I bet the Pilgrims would have loved ice cream. Back in their time, it hadn't been invented.

Mom

Grandma

Me

Grandpa

Our Thanksgiving

Here's my dad after a big Thanksgiving dinner. →

Dad ←

my brother ←

my sister →

What I'd Tell the Pilgrims

I'd like to tell the Pilgrims how everybody in America thinks of them at Thanksgiving time. I read that it's the most popular holiday we have. People travel from far away to get home. Families have big turkey dinners together. Everybody thinks about things they are thankful for. And the Pilgrims started it all! I'm thankful that they did.

Guess how many feathers a turkey has—3,500!

Americans eat 45 million turkeys every Thanksgiving!

Great job, Carrie. I learned a lot! Here is one more turkey fact—only males gobble. Female turkeys make a clicking soun
Ms. Brandt